AF414959
Would You Rather?
VOLUME 2
Gross Out Edition
150 Totally Disgusting Questions For Kids
J.L. Gee

j.l.gee
books

This Book Belongs To:

HEY KIDS!

Be smart, okay?
This book is for
entertainment only!
PLEASE DO NOT
ATTEMPT ANY OF THE
ACTIONS DESCRIBED
IN THIS BOOK!

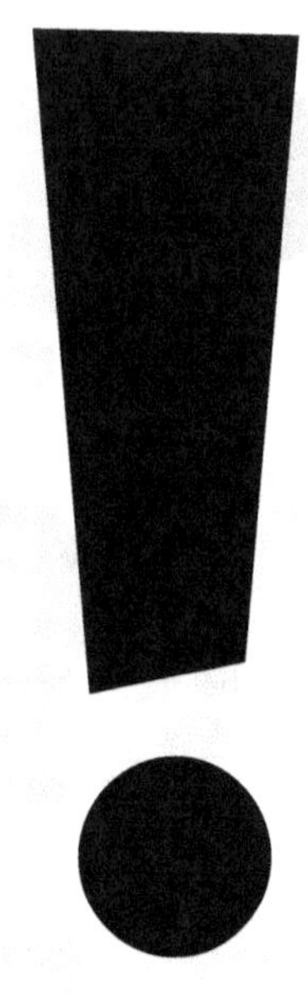

Ask your friends...
Ask your sibling...
Or ask yourself!

The only rule is the
person who answers
MUST pick one of the two
options.

HAVE FUN!

Would You Rather...

Have a baby poop
on you or throw up
on you?

Eat a giant spider
web or drink from a
mud puddle?

Would You Rather...

Spend the night in a dog house or on the floor of a public restroom?

Always smell like a skunk or like onions?

Would You Rather...

Wear someone else's dirty underwear or no underwear at all?
Lick a dead fish or a live fish?

Would You Rather...

Eat toenail clippings or spoiled food from a trash can?

Lick the bottom of your shoe or the door handle in a public building?

Would You Rather...

Still be bathed by your mother or your grandmother?

Sleep in a bed full of bedbugs or fire ants?

Would You Rather...

Eat a raw onion or a clove of raw garlic?

Never wash your hair again or never brush your teeth again?

Would You Rather...

Fart every 10 minutes or belch every time you try to talk?

Eat a chunk of hair or drink a glass of sweat?

Would You Rather...

Drink a glass of expired milk or eat a bowl of moldy fruit?

Have diarrhea in front of a stranger or your best friend?

Would You Rather...

Have to live with
your English teacher
or your math teacher
for a week?

Participate in gym class
wearing only your
underwear or someone
else's sweaty gym
clothes?

Would You Rather...

Eat chocolate flavored poop or poop flavored chocolate?

Always have sweaty armpits or sweaty butt cheeks?

Would You Rather...

Use a stranger's toothbrush or used dental floss?

Kiss your sibling or a rabid raccoon?

Would You Rather...

Be constantly itchy
or sticky?

Spend a week
wearing wet socks or
wet underwear?

Would You Rather...

Eat poison ivy or a handful of bees?

Poop your pants once in public or every day of your life in private?

Would You Rather...

Eat a whole jar of mayonnaise or a whole tub of butter?

Die by zombie attack or shark attack?

Would You Rather...

Sit in a tub filled with cockroaches or ants?

Have your tongue pulled out or one eyeball plucked out?

Would You Rather...

Hug a flea-infested dog or a full-grown buffalo?

Lick a public toilet seat or a stranger's armpit?

Would You Rather...

Eat your own
boogers or earwax?

Have wet cat food or
dry dog food for
dinner every night?

Would You Rather...

Have a non-itchy rash where people can see it or an itchy rash where people can't see it?

Always have bad breath or body odor?

Would You Rather...

Throw up on your best friend or have your best friend throw up on you?

Eat spaghetti made from worms or from hair?

Would You Rather...

Have people see you
in your underwear or
be able to read your
mind?

Swim through a
pool of eels or
jellyfish?

Would You Rather...

Pick your friend's nose
or cut your friend's
toenails?

Have asparagus
growing from your ears
or broccoli growing from
your butt?

Would You Rather...

Smell like cheese puffs
or spoiled milk?

Live in a dirty barn
with a friendly horse
or a clean barn with a
mean horse?

Would You Rather...

Find a stranger using your bathroom or sleeping in your bed?

Take a shower with a porcupine or a badger?

Would You Rather...

Swim in a pool filled with spoiled milk or spoiled mayonnaise?

Eat a pizza covered in live worms or dead cockroaches?

Would You Rather...

Spend the night in a porta-potty or eat dinner in dirty gas station bathroom?

Swim in a pool someone peed in or play in a sandbox filled with cat poop?

Would You Rather...

Drink a raw fish smoothie or eat a deep fried mouse?

Have a pet cockroach or a pet dung beetle?

Would You Rather...

Shave your best friend's legs or scratch their butt?

Have really stinky gas or really loud gas?

Would You Rather...

Never use soap again or never use shampoo again?

Wake up with a tarantula or a snake in your bed?

Would You Rather...

Pull out all your hair
one piece at a time or
in big chunks?

Try to hug an angry
kangaroo or an angry
stingray?

Would You Rather...

Be trapped in the earwax or booger of a giant?

Have a giant pimple on your nose or on your forehead for the rest of your life?

Would You Rather...

Never have clean bedsheets or clean socks?

Eat the contents of a vacuum or drink dirty mop water?

Would You Rather...

Your teacher come to your home every night for dinner or your parents come to school every day for lunch?

Have nose hair or ear hair that is long enough to braid?

Would You Rather...

Have a pie smashed in your face or be sprayed all over with silly string?

Have to sleep in the same bed as your sibling or a stranger?

Would You Rather...

Eat a hotdog or hamburger covered in chocolate pudding?

Have to drink all your beverages from a bucket or a baby bottle?

Would You Rather...

Shave your head with a rusty razor or pull out your teeth with rusty pliers?

Spin in circles or eat ice cream until you puke?

Would You Rather...

Have to share a
bedroom with 10
siblings or 1000 bees?

Always have to poop
in a litter box or your
backyard?

Would You Rather...

Take a bath in honey or a shower in maple syrup?

Eat booger flavored ice cream or ice cream flavored boogers?

Would You Rather...

Walk barefoot through poison ivy or horse poop?

Find a mouse in your box of cereal or flies in your carton of milk?

Would You Rather...

Be chased by 10
stinky skunks or 100
aggressive bees?

Have hair full of
lice or underwear
full of fleas?

Would You Rather...

Always have a bad
haircut or bad breath?

Walk 10 miles in
shoes filled with
pudding or mustard?

Would You Rather...

Get stuck in an elevator with a vampire bat or a pack of angry squirrels?

Stand in a bucket of ranch dressing in the hot sun or swim in a pool of barbecue sauce?

Would You Rather...

Walk to school barefoot in cold snow or on hot concrete?

Be stranded on an island with an alien or a werewolf?

Would You Rather...

Turn into a cranky goat
or a stubborn mule?

Get buried up to your
neck in snow or in sand?

Would You Rather...

Only be allowed to drink warm water or cold, black coffee for the rest of your life?

Eat three slimy worms or a peanut butter and fish stick sandwich?

Would You Rather...

Be stung with 1000 bees
or eat 1000 bees?

Always feel like you
have to sneeze or like
you have to poop?

Would You Rather...

Drink a cup of toilet water or a gallon of hot sauce?

Always have super chapped lips or really bad dandruff?

Would You Rather...

Squirt lemon juice in your eyes or eat a whole ghost pepper?

Drink your best friend's backwash or eat their chewed food?

Would You Rather...

Pee your bed every
night or pee your pants
in school once?

Be constantly itchy or
always have to cough?

Would You Rather...

Have to groom a grizzly bear or brush a tiger's teeth?

Use sandpaper as toilet paper or use hot sauce as eye drops?

Would You Rather...

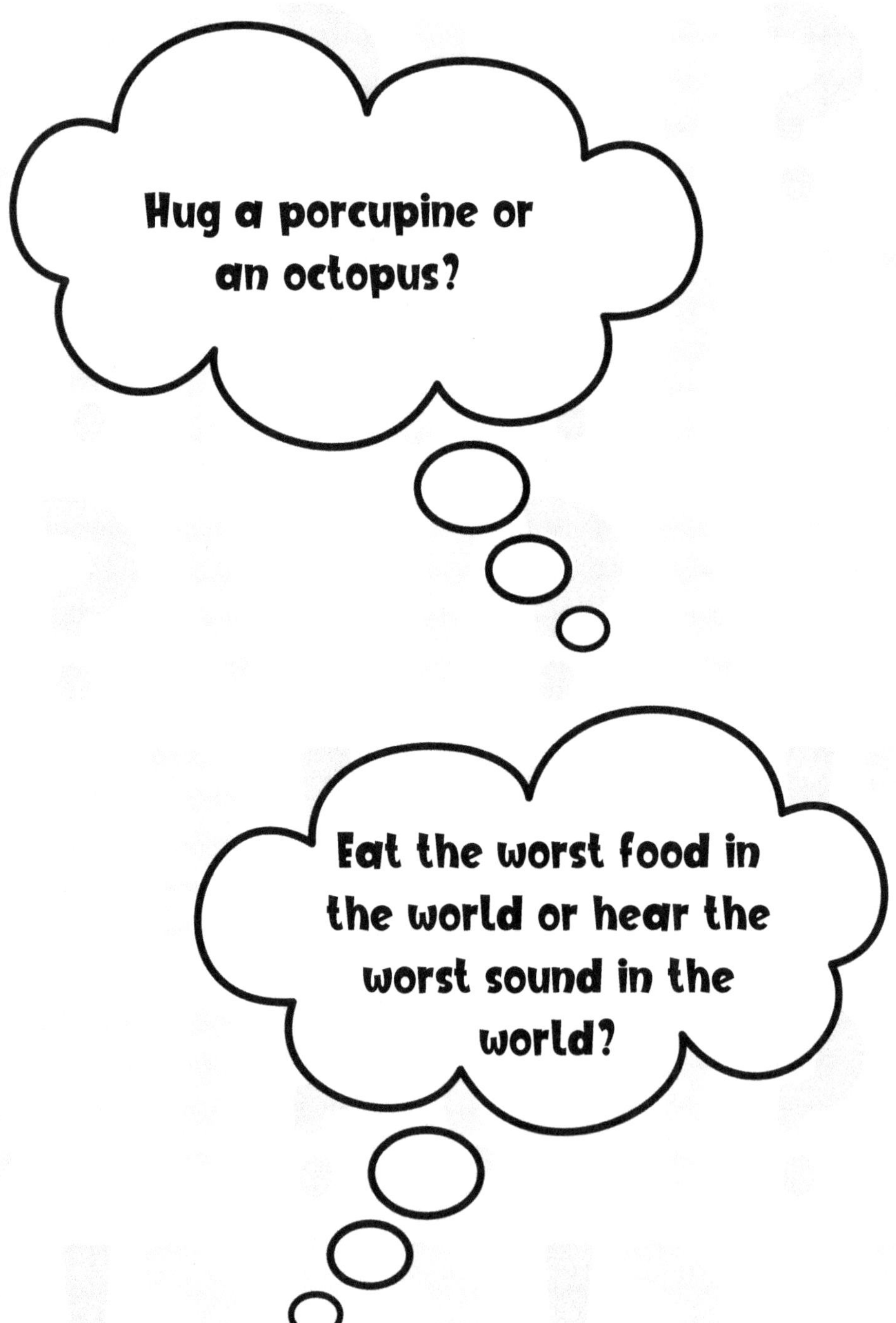

Hug a porcupine or an octopus?

Eat the worst food in the world or hear the worst sound in the world?

Would You Rather...

Eat weird tasting
food or wear weird
looking clothes?

Take a bath in ice
or jello?

Would You Rather...

Go to school in your underwear or walk barefoot through the snow?

Eat a stick of butter or a bottle of mustard?

Would You Rather...

Be covered head to
toe in hair or
completely hairless?

Get stuck in a storm
of glitter or orange
juice?

Would You Rather...

Spend the night in a haunted house or creepy cave?

Eat brussels sprout ice cream or broccoli cake?

Would You Rather...

Be kidnapped by a supervillain or a wicked witch?

Lick a frog or eat a stink bug?

Would You Rather...

Eat garbage like a
stray dog or slop
like a pig?

Have snake scales or
duck feathers?

Would You Rather...

Be spit on by a
camel or sprayed by
a skunk?

Step on a Lego or
get gum stuck in
your hair?

Would You Rather...

Be allergic to your favorite food or your favorite animal?

Have witch hands or alien skin?

Would You Rather...

Have greasy hair
down to your ankles
or be totally bald?

Have hair made of
earthworms or a
shirt made of fish
scales?

Would You Rather...

Sleep on a bed of pumpkin guts or cold spaghetti noodles?

Be constipated for the rest of your life or have to poop every hour?

Would You Rather...

Have your mom drop you off at school in her bathrobe or kiss you goodbye in front of your friends?

Live in a house full of bugs or mice?

Would You Rather...

Find a cockroach in your candy bar or a dead slug in your soda?

Jump into a ball pit with dirty diapers or go down a slide with poop smeared on it?

Would You Rather...

Have to share a bed with your parents or your grandparents?

Use a backpack your cat peed on or wear sneakers with dog poop on them?

Would You Rather...

Have snakes inside your mattress or rats covering your bedroom floor?

Have a runny nose that never stops or permanent bad breath?

Would You Rather...

Smell like garlic or
sour milk?

Swim with sharks or
run with bulls?

Would You Rather...

Get bit by a snake or stung by a jellyfish?

Get stung by a bee or get a bad sunburn?

Would You Rather...

Be stuck in a balloon full of helium or water?

Eat a spoonful of sand or drink a mud smoothie?

Would You Rather...

Jump rope barefoot on
hot coals or slip and
slide on a mat covered
in dog pee?

Live a year in a
cave in the forest or
in a tent in the
jungle?

Would You Rather...

Be covered in bee stings or mosquito bites?

Spend a day with sand in your swimsuit or rocks in your shoes?

Would You Rather...

Drink a witch's potion or watch a scary movie?

Have your dog turn into a wolf or your cat turn into a tiger?

Would You Rather...

Be sat on by a sumo wrestler or tackled by an NFL player?

Slather your body in cream cheese or marshmallow fluff?

Would You Rather...

Eat your dinner out of a litter box or a dirty diaper?

Play catch with a hornet nest or a soccer ball covered in dog poop?

Would You Rather...

Slurp a raw egg
through a straw or
swallow a live
goldfish?

Top your pizza with
fireplace ashes or
shower drain hair?

Would You Rather...

Swim in a septic tank or dunk your head in a toilet?

Have someone sneeze in your mouth or clean their shoe with your toothbrush?

Would You Rather...

Have your mom as
your teacher or your
principal?

Eat a dog booger or
a cat hairball?

Like this book?

Please review it on Amazon!

Find more books by J.L. Gee at

jlgeebooks.com

Until next time...

~ J.L. Gee